GLASS JAW

GLASS

POEMS

JAW

RAISA TOLCHINSKY

A KAREN & MICHAEL BRAZILLER BOOK

PERSEA BOOKS / NEW YORK

Persea Books, Inc.
90 Broad Street
New York, New York 10004

Library of Congress Cataloging-in-Publication Data

Names: Tolchinsky, Raisa, author.
Title: Glass jaw : poems / Raisa Tolchinsky.
Description: New York : Persea Books, 2024. | "A Karen & Michael Braziller Book." | Summary: "Winner of the 2023 Lexi Rudnitsky First Book Prize in Poetry, Glass Jaw is a gripping, Dantaen rendering of a young woman's physical and spiritual trials in the boxing ring"— Provided by publisher.
Identifiers: LCCN 2023054089 (print) | LCCN 2023054090 (ebook) | ISBN 9780892555796 (paperback ; acid-free paper) | ISBN 9780892555857 (epub)
Subjects: LCGFT: Poetry.
Classification: LCC PS3620.O32597 G57 2024 (print) | LCC PS3620.O32597 (ebook) | DDC 811/.6—dc23/eng/20231127
LC record available at https://lccn.loc.gov/2023054089
LC ebook record available at https://lccn.loc.gov/2023054090

Book design and composition by Rita Lascaro
Typeset in Carat
Manufactured in the United States of America. Printed on acid-free paper.

For those who have descended
and returned

CONTENTS

GLASS JAW

DIATRIBE ON
WOMEN GLADIATORS

"How can a woman be decent,
sticking her head in a helmet,
denying the sex she was born with?"

—JUVENAL, *SATIRE VI*

I'm not sure why I still pray, or *how* I do it anymore. It's like knocking on the sky: *can a* girl come in? I knock with my whole body: which *woman* is made of engine grease and hot hands? All of them, although *"be decent"* is the first rule of God. I'm *sticking* to it but I should tell you the first woman did not eat the apple but threw it. *Her* apple had teeth marks. It rolled like a *head* across the muddy field and rooted down. *In* me the arsenic sprouted a world made from a catapult. The apple was *a* satellite, orbiting, a *helmet* protecting nothing. The apple was a Lilith *denying* she ever took a bite. There it is: the orchard where she said *the* word for the first time: *sex*, that snakelike hiss, and owned it O the rattlesnake came, wriggling. *She* bent her head toward me, flicked a forked tongue, and *was* not afraid. Or, did the snake speak? A cord wrapped around us. Be *born* again but this time, take everything *with*

Anna
[Bless the Boxing Ring]

The crook and knot of hand, how I reached out and spun myself

dreidel in red dust until I rose from and lifted into armor, dissipating

coin, rusted nail. Bless this underworld of secret choir. Singing punches,

sideways limbs. The dawn I saved away every day for a year. Spin.

My shoulders that have not left me. Yes, *I can do hard things*. Bless

the hard things. My first punch that landed. The lights in my own eyes.

So small when I twirled in flattened fields, dizzied by sky. Bless the choice

to cross my own rope: twenty-two square feet of skin, stadium of blushing heart.

Bless the iron in my body, enough to make a nail. The salt fact of me.

My tongue, the strongest muscle I own. The flickering flame of my mouth

that will not go out.

Delia

[The Trick Is Vick's Vaporub, Salt,
and Yellow Foundation]

I smile at what I made. It blooms
on your left cheek as you say *goddamn*
and circle its red rim with gold,

then powder, then slick lotion
up your legs. Tony is right
through the double doors

crying his eyes out of the tear duct
that still works. In here,
we don't owe him anything,

mirror and hydrangeas,
blood and white tea eau de toilette,
pantyhose, blazer slicked back

ponytail so convincing I almost forget
your jab in the first round stung
my cheek into a smile. I love you,

all of you and your 100 uppercuts
to the gut I got for Christmas—
that's the deal and I don't mind

your hands my ribs your mouth
(my mouth, we don't speak of that).
We don't speak in the ring except for

get up but in here the music is so loud
they can't hear us over the *millonario yo,
millonario con quien ando* comparing mascaras

all clump from the sweat
and would we still do this,
if we were millionaires?

Carmen
[You're a Woman Until You Spit Twice in the Bucket]

Now the audience
wants you to be a woman
plus a floor of shattered plates,
a broken window, a hidden belt
that won't stop whipping itself
into a swollen eye.
The audience wants whiplash,
wants a mouthpiece slick with blood,
a few loose teeth
and applause loud enough to crack a beer bottle.

Then, they want silence.
They want you crying in the corner like a still-life—
a vase,
a bonnet,
a little bird.

The opposite of "catcher's mitt" is "*how* do I knock an opponent out?" The opposite of "*can a* fight never end" is "*woman.*" You don't believe me? *Be* very still and watch—it's not *decent* to kill in the ring, unlike UFC, where you can get away with *sticking* your hands anywhere you want. We're regal here. *Her* honor matters, even if she'll take your *head* and call it a dance. Dance, the audience says, and the ring *in a* cold winter becomes a guillotine. You're wearing a *helmet*—won't matter when the blade comes. Stop *denying* you're afraid. I've done it my whole life with *spandex* wrapped around my waist. I want them to say *she was* a most terrifying kind of beauty: *born* to keep killing, her lipstick covered *with* glass.

Melissa
[Compared to Boxing, Labor Was Easy]

Three hours past dawn
I begged for numbness
though for years I had
trained for the kind of pain

     that shakes a body open.

Before you I was not afraid:
my own death just a fleck
of glitter on the cheek
glinting at me in the mirror

     but only after I had been hit

hard enough to see twinkling
at the edges of my vision—
the blue hum of a concussion
no lullaby I would ever want to sing.

     Daughter, I had felt pain

but never pain that made way
for something beyond it
and it terrified me, the numbness,
how it felt like rest—

     which Coach said always

arrived empty-handed,
didn't win any prizes or belts.

     What hurt the most?

Seeing
for the first time
your hands

so small
already curled
into fists

Esther
[Some Things You Can't Understand by Punching Harder]

I blushed like I had already been hit when she slipped that cotton baton
into my pocket between bells, though why was I ashamed our bodies emptied

without breaking? I rinsed blood from my hands and Coach parted the ropes.
Make him forget what you are. We never sparred the boys yet

he looked at me like the rib we had stolen was between my eyes.
Then hit so hard I heard a sound like fishing hooks in a drawstring bag

(no one really sees stars glittering above them, the dark begins at the ankles, then
zips up)—he waited to say *I can't hit a girl* until I was already on the ground.

What ails you, that you flee? O Jordan, that you turn back?

Most of the boys had seen a body bleed almost everywhere a body could
and never did I see them wince: not at the tooth wedged into the mat,

or the face shifted into a Picasso painting, or a pupil pummeled red.
Still, the fight stopped quick as the moment

God returned the Red Sea only to part it again.
What are the rules for that?

Kate

chest

                              shoulder

head   torso   hands

breath

            hands   cheek

                                        hands
breath

        mouth

                        hips
hands

                hands

Even the days bleed like cuts. Riddle me this: *How* come time slows before a fight? How *can a* clock keep breaking before the bell? Call this *"woman*'s work" because no one has the words for how it feels to *be* bloody in your mind. It's a *descent* into a basement, *sticking* your hand into a little box with an animal you can't see. Let's call *her* "little woman," the coaches said, patting my pummeled *head*. I etched the words "let me *in*" onto my tongue, but it didn't matter. What's it to you? What's a girl without a first kiss? Without a fist? What's a headless horseman with *a helmet*? Safety is a myth, I'll tell my daughter, if I have one. Safety is *denying* how we're always in a basement looking for the light. The truth is, a good punch is better than *the* best *sex* I've ever had. I've heard what they said: *"she was* damned until she wrapped her hands." But they felt *born* again to me when I clenched them, wondering, what comes *with*?

Arya
[Snail Mail]

The promoter runs on Red Bull, smells like drugstore cologne. In his spare time he makes collages out of $20 bills; shoots a BB gun at pigeons. Most notably, the promoter likes to smash things in his sleep: watches, dishware, glass figurines. After the fight, he drapes a wet hand across my shoulder and says *I know what you want.* I say, *I want a fence no one can cross. I want a snow globe that won't stop snowing. I want my palms pink and uncalloused as my inner ear.* Two weeks later, I get a package. It's filled with shards of glass. There's a note: *if you use them to mark your problem spots, maybe you can be a ring girl.* There's no return address but I know who it's from. He always signs his checks with a single X just to see if they'll go through.

Kira

[Once I Was a Ring Girl, Too]

Saw blood spilling from mouths
saw left hook to the body
left hook to the head
head body head body
and no matter the outcome
I held those cards
high, cocked a hip
still sore from training
the day before.
For so long
it was the only
way they'd let
me inside the ring.
But that night,
it was me
with my head
busted open
in the ring girl's lap—
blood's slow trickle
pooling
in the sequins
of her dress
and my god, her skin
without bruises:
phosphorescent.
I held her hand
as she drove
me home
even my pinky finger
crooked.
In the ring
they called us
different names
but we were
both inside it
until we weren't:

outside my house
she pressed
her mouth to mine
still bleeding
from the fight
and for a moment
with my title belt
sparkling under all
those streetlights
I felt like I could love
her like a person
instead of a fighter
in between rounds.

Midnight dark is my friend. I light my candles and pray: show me *how*, but I know the answer. *Can a* bruise be breakfast? I'll dig and dig for a *woman* as afraid as me who keeps fighting. "Just let it *be*" sing The Beatles on the jukebox as we spar, and then Coach says: "You're lookin *decent*," but he wrings his hands, eyes *sticking* to her instead of me. What does she have that I don't? Her smile still whole, her manicured hands. "Put *her head* on a platter," Coach says, grinning, but his eyes twist *in a* time-capsule: it's myself 10 years ago. No headgear, no *helmet*—that's how you can tell who's new. It's simple, *denying* what will hurt you. It's simple, pretending *the sex* you have won't waste your win. *She was* so stupid, I heard myself say about myself. Born wild, said my mother, *born with* her hands in fists.

Samiya

[Years ago I lost]

Pain knits
itself new shapes.
Not clouds
but neurons.
They drag
their wired
tails across
the center
of my mind.

Alex
[Circling the Ring]

When I look into Sammy's eyes I can't tell if he sees me or not so I speak to him like a dog, say, *good boy,* cluck hard and fast so he knows where to put his body: sixteen hands tall, legs veiny as a maple leaf, thorough-bred and made for racing. *What's it like to lead a thing that big,* I ask Jillian, the instructor. She's under five feet but Sammy believes she's big as a house. *They like to be ridden,* Jillian says, though at first I feel almost guilty when she pries open his mouth, tightens the girth. Saddled up, I expect him to rear to his full height, shake me off into the dust. Instead he stands still, waiting patiently. I want to ask him, don't you know what you could do? Once I met a dominatrix. She had feet the size of a child's. In one hand she held a glass of champagne and in the other, a leash attached to a man six feet tall. His face was so gentle when he called her *mistress*—like a prayer. She winked at me when I walked in on her in the dungeon bathroom, brushing her hair. She said, *Honey, you could do what I do, if you wanted. Do you want to beat me up,* a man once asked. I didn't answer, so when I was least expecting it, he wrapped a hand around my throat: *Gotchya. Sammy is a good horse,* says Jillian. He's a thoroughbred, made for running as fast as he can, but between my legs, he's slow as a cow—I make him walk in circles, just because I can.

Coach X.
[Interview]

the taste
of blood
and grief
that lingers
spins the
perimeter
of my body
already busted
open by
shampoo bottles
sugar cubes
coffee cups
a china patterned
plate
a foot a head
a fist a fist
which is why
when i was eight
i promised myself
i'd grow up
to be the kind
of superhero
who lived wide
and filled with
woman
like wolverine
who when
the police said
*put your weapons
down* said *i can't*
and held up
his hands
long blades
covered in skin
and god bless him,
his weapons

were indistinguishable
from song
for a moment,
unbloomed roses

Jess
[It Does Not Matter]

It does not matter my friend can throw a punch or that her superman kick can put a six foot man on the ground. I am always waiting for this call. I'm always thinking about alleys, guns, boys we call our best friends until. There is no poetry in that. There is no perfect day in green grass, dragonflies, jumping rope in Astoria Park. A girl grins at me across the track while I shadowbox. She's seven or eight. She wants to know how to throw a jab, a hook, an uppercut. I'll show her though I want to make her promise a list of things she won't do but I don't want her to be careful. I want her to flick her fists into the sun like she's strong enough to dent it. I want her to make the sun a donut and look through it into another world where my friend has never called me today, weeping, where I have not had to wonder what it is I must say. I watch this girl's fists, the first of autumn caught in her hair. "Thumbs down," I say, "like this like this like this."

I didn't stop to ask *how* once I saw the two pink lines I just asked, *can a* mother be a mother and a fighter both, can a *woman* mother herself into a form of *Be*ing that hardens and softens into *decent* work: to be called "baby" then give birth, to wipe the *stickiness* off your daughter's hands, to ring-a-round a rosie to ring-a-round the ring and oh *her* laughter matters so much you forget your throbbing *head* and the sound of muscle *in a* corridor of pain and *hell* already *met*—if they ask if you're a mother, *deny*, say "I'm my own," say *sex* without child though your body was watched for weight then daughter, though *she was* never yours, she was first-*born* to an audience who chooses who lives forged, who survives as *w*ordsm*ith*

Purgatory

We're trying to say
we've watched our
bodies without us
in them. Called ourselves
orphan, coiling
through the world.
In the field we played
with pebbles like
children and made
bargains with a bold
God. We thought if
we built what haunted us
a cage we could touch it
and survive

Purgatory

In a field, the coaches kneel before us
in our baby pink pantsuits and we bless their hands with roses.
We carry thorns in our pockets
from all the times we spit out mouthpieces
soaked in spit, some man yelling:
what that mouth do?
while we hunched drooling, over the bucket.
O, knot after knot after knot. They should have asked
for forgiveness before they killed us
with push-ups, sit-ups, goblin squats.
Now birds hover around our bulked-up
shoulders. How holy we are with our hair undone—
spread your wings: flamingo, rosefinch, robin.
Nest between our healed knuckles
as the coaches write their prayers
on hand wraps, unscrolling across our field
of allium bloom. No one gave them permission
to enter. X. arrives first, offers film canisters of skunky
Ghost Train, Bruce Banner, caffeine pills. He rolls a joint,
wants forgiveness from his father. Y appears on his
motorized scooter, in love with a girl who
left. I know about the nowhere
he won't go back to, not even for Thanksgiving.
Z is the hardest to bear. What hasn't he done?
He's got the fastest hands. He wants forgiveness
and we don't blame him. He hands over a tupperware
of tunafish sandwiches. *Please*—he says.
We'll consider it. We sit at our long table
and pour the wine. You can get the next one, we say, re-filling their glasses.
The coaches swallow every drop like they have nothing to fear.
They think the hard work is done, but we'll make them watch
the sun sink below the horizon (the only rope allowed)
as the sky turns pink pink pink—our favorite Pepto-Bismal
ballerina, our favorite bubble gum that burns.

● ● ●

HERE THIS
HOLLOW SPACE

oh where have you fallen to
son of the morning
beautiful lucifer
—LUCILLE CLIFTON

And now—with fear
I set it down in meter
—DANTE ALIGHIERI

Canto 34
Before Dawn, With the Street Lamp's
Beam Across Your Face

When you dream you dream red
an open palm an ocean which takes you swinging
your legs out of bed bruised as if with hammers
packing your bag with the lights off putting in things
that don't belong: butterfly wing, lock of hair, opal rattle
of your mind—you ask for help, you pray
to spell your own name with biceps, shoulders,
breath and if the sky looks like a wound,
what does that say about you? It's blue
as your upper thigh as the sun rises, lowers
you down the subway's wet steps:
puddled urine, sour rain, everything a cave
a grave of you and construction workers,
the midnight shift coming home,
eying your pink boxing bag—you wear it like
a bulletproof vest in the train filled with birds.
Now the sky the lightest pink.
Now you are not a girl walking through the park
but a myth preparing for an ending
bell then a (*get up, who said you could rest*)—the gym door
broken, shattered with glass as you write
down your name, flat clipboard: I was here, again
down the stairs to the basement covered in posters of men
with rutted faces, some of them still alive
with the sound of hard work happening before you see it:
thwack of mitt against pad, hard breath, jump rope stinging
linoleum, and the bell that never turns off, sweet swinging silver
pendulum that will keep ticking even after you quit
though you haven't quit yet—the rest of the girls are in the ring
already but you're late on purpose, you're afraid you're afraid
of too much time inside—*how you doin, Queen of Roses,*
Rodrick says, famous coach who asked what your name meant
and you told him, though you almost lied—*Queen of Roses, roses, roses*—
two doors in the locker room keeping the sounds out—*where are your thorns?*

Sometimes Mia is there, or Alex, smelling like expensive perfume.
They bring their own hairdryers, lipstick, powder. Ponytails smoothed
back, scuffed boxing shoes, lace under everything until they armor up
and strap down. Mia always shows her six pack (*the coaches are bored,*
she says, *entertain them from far away*
and they'll leave you alone)—but you pull
your hoodie over your headphones, tie your shoes tight.
Jumprope, headgear, hand-wraps—
good luck out there, Andy says, winking.
She's got a three year old she brings in
to watch her spar—*watch what mommy does,*
you're next, next, the jump rope, three rounds, but you trip
when Marco comes over and says *will you go on a date with me?*
and you say *Marco, no a thousand times no* but he circles as you double-under
cross-over and whip yourself with rope and Rodrick yells, *Marco, leave her alone*
while you drop into a plank, planking until Cristian puts a foot on your back
and says *stay strong,* two minutes left, and the burning, and Cristian's foot
pressing down—so (you choose this, don't you?)
when you finally get up to shadowbox, you punch the air so hard
you hear a whistling and *what you so angry about, girl,*
another coach asks from across the room and you smile
whenever they speak to you: *Do you have a boyfriend?*
What do you do for work? How many rounds?—easier
to give away nothing but teeth in a land
of sweat and leather and sewage; ten rounds on the heavy bag with two
kinds of pain, dull and hot. You feel both,
and time stretches until your shoulders give.
Oh, bells. The Gatorade, red.
The locker room, emptied.
You catch your breath, watch your red
face in the mirror. Swipe of lipstick and a pencil skirt,
heels and perfume. Soon you'll pour water for business men
as they lunch. You'll smile and ask, *how can I help you?*
You'll hide (hide them!) your scabbed hands.

Canto 33
Can I Write This?

I ask every friend.
A. says yes
against the rain
says *speak it* when
his weathered ghost
arrives in our bed,
face cratered with letters I've flung
to make him visible,
her lips slow along the corridor
of my throat
as if to let me let him go
in sound I am not proud of
no words but guttural
not lit with smile or smoothed over
but crazed my face in the shadows she says
the surface of a frozen lake
she cannot touch

Canto 32
I Rewind It

I don't get in the cab.
I don't open the door.
I say *no* until my no breaks open—
flies swarm from
where the little mouth
hangs. They land on his face
and his arms tanned by sun,
and bite down. All day,
tang in the mouth.

Canto 31
My Black Underwear Hangs above the Lemon Trees

(Cinque Terre)

I arrange each one to hide the stains.
Here I could be anybody
and have not loved him,
never waited on my knees
or woken to a rumpled bed.
Instead, I drink espresso,
pin up my hair, let strange
golden men light my cigarettes
with a quick flick of the wrist.
I don't smoke but look
what their hands can do.
No fist but fire and breath.
I bend down to peer below the sea—
a bloated fish swims in circles.
All this light and still a gaping mouth,
a door that never closes.

Canto 30
I Became within My Speechlessness

December at the cafe with Giana
the oak table between us
once tall and green and breathing
but *nothing happened,* I say,
that I didn't agree to,
his hands on my waist,
two glasses of whiskey
and dimmed lights.
What's an agreement? Giana asks.
Her hair is the color of the moon.
She's not afraid of the axe of my shame:
oh, I should have known.

Canto 29
A Knife Scrapes off the Scales

As I recount this I wonder
if it's right, or if still his hand corrects
my hand the way it did for years—
bending my wrist or fingers
to *punch like you're pouring*
a pitcher of water
down the drain.
Often, evenings
when I pick up a pencil
or unlock the door,
the motion wakes
a muscle that memorized
his face—obsession
a motor task
written into my
movement
for he lives in me
but is not here—
just a memory
I repeat to myself
just a slant of light—
though his shadow
itches even
this page,
where I make his face
bloom again, then erase it.
I scratch
until the paper
tears. Each word's
mirror I turn to the wall,
then look again
to see—

Canto 29
From July until September

Easier if there were no
fractals of joy
weaving through the blight:
chin chin, ossifying
our wine glasses
across the table,
his dog's soft head
in my lap.
Or how he bent down
to adjust my sneakered feet
as if in worship.
So neat and tidy
it would be
if I could forget
how much he wanted me to win.

Canto 28
Carried by the Hair, the Severed Head

A loop can be fashioned from anything,
even snow, sunshine, a song—
right round baby, right round
cheery *Dead or Alive* ear-worm as I paced
my cabin and saw again
the girl I was who kept walking
and never spoke his name.
In two, I split, and then in hundreds,
the girls who could have left but instead
loafed about in vantablack lace.
In quick circles I walked them
until they dizzied and clawed
on that conveyer belt
I stuck myself inside and spun.
Home in Astoria, I expected
the stale swing of his call.
Where you been. Did I stumble
up the stairs to his apartment
as I practiced saying what I'd said
alone for weeks? *I'm going to leave.*
But to leave means also to unfurl—
trees leaved, wild-flowers, too.
I meant both meanings against his chest
as I spoke my careful sentence,
my head swiveling in slow rounds—
While you were gone, did you write about me?
Coach asked, but I could hear no music.

Canto 27
No Exit

(Laugarvatn, Iceland)

The dark that was promised to me
was not there instead the sun
hovering three fingers above
the horizon line—my mind's blue-black
spotlight even during blizzards
the twenty minutes to town
for jumprope, pushups,
three rounds of shadowbox
where my long underwear iced
beneath my clothes.
Everywhere I went I was
the ring I peered into,
longing for my own
sunlit face I found him
in front of me, behind me,
angled to the side—
I'd waited for the Northern Lights
all my life. But I was not alone
under that green pirouetting sky.
I had been fighting for so long,
I could see through my hands—
straight to their steak-lashed muscle,
straight to the snowy bone.

Canto 26
Within Those Fires, There Are Souls

Before the ring I made a life out of language
but there were places it would not reach—
the ring needed no words, no stone
to crown me in concussion
until I had no energy left to speak.
How many nights did I stand on my roof
stunned silent underneath a grey starless sky?
The story became the angler's lure,
and I the angler, reaching for that pinprick in the dark—
not Coach but who I was as I told what happened—
What happened? Who am I, here?
Tea-kettle in my jaw so loud
I forgot the flame. I forgot the pot heating slowly
and the frog, rattling the lid.

Canto 25
Two Intermingled Shapes Appeared

Slam slam went the door in my chest,
as it had for twenty-two years. Slam slam,
high school, changing out of my PE uniform
hips straightened back to a slash.
I saw a girl's flesh marked with sapphires,
a belt's red stripe across her throat.
Why, I thought—pity a chasm I would not cross
or couldn't, because I was already
in the rift. If Coach—if he ever—outside of the ring—
I would have considered it
self-flagellation. In the bodega's windows,
I saw his reflection instead of my own:
hands on my hips, his pose—
Enough time with him
and what would I become?
Dogs begin to smile the same way
as their owners. Those long hours watching
him slap the speed-bag into the wall,
space around us like a moat.
When I was near him, men bowed their heads
and never reached out to touch—
I exhaled there, I expanded.

Canto 24
On Seeing

So you thought you were special?
asked a fighter in the locker-room
smoothing lotion up her legs until
even the bruises shined. *Sorry to break it
to you but this is just what he does.*
So casual, my new friend,
as she slung a muscled arm
around my shoulders and pointed:
her and her and her and her—
walking back out I tried to adjust
my eyes. In the floor to ceiling mirror,
they all looked a little like me—
this one lifting weights.
This one doing sit-ups, then writhing on the floor.
In a rom-com we'd hatch a plan, take over
the gym and leave him with nothing.
But then I saw their eyes, grey and filled with rot.
Was it then I vowed to put a stop to it,
to be different, to leave?
The problem was, I was mesmerized
by my own routine, soothed by the rhythm of the days:
egg whites, ice baths, acupuncture.
My gym, my job, my minutes filled.
Here were the hours for wringing my hands,
here were the hours for eating.
You'd never guess, said my new friend,
watching Coach fumble with the zipper
of his coat. I felt safe knowing where he was—
inside the day, not the tangle
of my mind. Christmas, Easter, birthdays.
Years like this? Years?

Canto 23
Were I a Leaded Mirror

The messages came in the night, two a.m. or later.
good that i'm a coward or i'd kill
myself my phone blinking through the night's pitch.
I was strong, remember? I ran towards that pit
as if I could pull him out, each morning
opening the gym doors to see if he'd still be alive.
Who was I supposed to call? His mother?
In the boxing ring, no one spoke of them.
Fathers, yes—their voices clanged across the years,
the ropes humming guitar strings.
Broken plates, open hands striking the face flat.
Who asks about the devil's father?
Did he wake into the world
or was he, too, handed a red coat to wear?
Coach's wish was to do less damage than was done to him.
He said *i'm a horrible person* so casual it pulled me closer
as as we sipped strawberry wine, sweetness
a pink noose around my throat—
It wouldn't be your fault, a wise woman said.
But when he watched me spar, each body I struck
was his body. I dare you, tell me I wasn't like his father:
each fist to the gut, what I needed to say
but couldn't.

Canto 22
Wings Were Not More Fast than Fear

The treadmill's long miles
moved me nowhere in the damp
of the basement
though it was Sunday and up above
the day was shining, the trees
unfurling into bloom—
Coach hadn't been around for weeks,
I was counting the days and watching
the mirrors behind me as if he'd suddenly appear
refracted and in multiple.
It was a new trainer who said
    faster, baby,
(his bruised cheek an apple too ugly to sell)
    good girl, move those legs
as I sped towards nothing except
   the pale heat
of my own exhaustion—no,
I don't want to make beautiful
how, stepping off the treadmill, this man
slapped my ass and finally said my name
    wrong which I answered to
by saying nothing, nothing until
stretched out behind the ring
on a mat salted white
with the sweat of strangers
   I arched my back
as if to bring
   the black pitch
that began in my center
up to the bricked room
   of my throat—

Canto 21
I Saw It, But I Could Not See within It

What of this was mine? What year was it, what day?
I have forgotten but still it plays:
now I write and speak and watch my tongue in the mirror
I've already half-covered. *Do not believe everything you see,*
said Arielle, who named what ate at her (until she did not eat)
Stacy. Little blonde disorder. She talked to it, too,
said *Stacy, I see you* (name it, before it names you)
but I did not know how to name what surged through me.
Certainly not Stacy. Not mother. Not murder.
Not chimney blowing the smoke back.
Not medicine. Not junkyard heart.
I can tell you in the end, it was not the devil
that haunted me. Most days, I got no text. He left me alone
with my churning and prayer shawls,
my Aramaic in the dead of night.
I thought I was divinely guided.
What else could have brought me
to a cold apartment on 30th street,
flat on my back in a spinning room?

Canto 20
I Was Well Prepared to Stare Below

The cards don't lie said Arielle
pushing her blue hair from her eyes
as we shuffled the deck during a break
between shifts, the coffee pot hissing
as we bent over the Major Arcana:
The Moon, The Sun, The High Priestess
gleaming on her pearl white throne.
I tugged on the sutures of the story
I had already lived. Again, I said, again,
until I pulled what I had hoped for
from the deck. When I cheated,
even The Tower (reversed)
was a good sign. Or The Star, pouring
from her lifted cup. I wiped tables
until my hands stung of bleach
but all the while I was a magician,
a hierophant, a fool.

Canto 19
We Had Already Reached the Tomb

Sasha once said sex
turns everything upside down,
contracts a man into
a black hole, a tunneling
kaleidoscopic twist
turning over the light
on the Brooklyn Bridge,
cocktails the color
of windex, Sasha's
echoing laugh
jewel-like and far away,
for nothing could reach me
feet flaming as I thrashed
trying to find a way to turn
myself right back up again,
a glimmering beetle in
summer's flat heat.
Years back the middle school boys
flicked insects onto their backs
to see how long it took them
to turn right side up:
trembling legs, wings
warped green glass against
the pavement's heat.
The boys placed bets
and their beetles won them
ice-cream sandwiches, once a condom
from some older brother.
Coach's timer hung from
his neck. I was better
than a beetle, a drinking bird,
an acrobat's flip.

Canto 18
With Polished Words

In the blue ditch of his bed
he carried no torch
to the bottom of that ravine
so I told him he was beautiful
and spun the syllables
of every empty bottle
into something like God—
here is our cathedral, I said,
though it smelled like an animal's stall—
I hummed a psalm
against his ripped ligaments
and twisted knee,
sucked the onyx smoke
from his lungs
until I could make no sound
each vocal chord chilled
then snapped, my laugh
filled with craters and gasp.
In the silence—was it loneliness?
No, it was not loneliness.
It was the devil's
whip against my rib:
I got to choose
the cord that lashed me.

Canto 17
I Felt the Threat of Shame,
Which Makes a Servant . . . Brave.

Coach kept changing shape—
devil, monster, minotaur
with rotted horns
but sometimes
a weeping man, dark curls
spilling across my lap—
or was it me who changed him
as I squinted my eyes
then handed over a paisley shirt?
I dressed him so bright his face blurred
and women with lips waxed red
craned their necks to see—
love, an unnatural angle,
how we sipped Coca Colas
on Sunday afternoons and watched
the swans in Central Park
swim in circles for so long
I forgot his iron fists, barbed tail
tucked in its cabinet—
even the ugliest angler fish
is beautiful
if you're only looking at its lure.

Canto 16
Around My Waist I Had a Cord

Mouthfuls of abrasion begin to taste
like wine gone sour, fuzzing the mind,
each morning my bleating alarm just one
in a series of bells. Upon waking
I reached for an Advil pink as dawn,
a salve to spread on the newest bruise.
How many times was I hit?
How many pounds per square inch? I forget
to make a cure, first you must identify the pain.
Does it split the side open, or stun
the nerve until it stills?
Blue vervain, arnica, comfrey distilled—
tinctures thick as honey for
my sparring partners
whose injuries swelled,
subsided, and never went away.
I made the cure so I knew where to hit.
Fair is fair—everyone knew to aim for my soft upper lip
that burst into bloom during almost every match.
Bleeding, how many times did I say *sorry*
but in the slur: *quarry, quarry*
which means a pit
just as it means prey

Canto 15
That Spirit Having Stretched His Arm Toward Me

How many sunsets
split the sky red
and I did not think
twice about the color?
That summer in the salt flats,
hiking in circles—
thirty days watching
thirty spattered skies fade
above the knotted land,
my tent just a gold rip
in endless black.
One morning I woke
to a sign a fellow hiker
staked, then walked on
—*land of the dead*—
I was seventeen. If I peered
hard enough
into a horizon's
shimmering heat,
would I have seen Coach
jogging parallel,
barely breaking a sweat
in his blue track suit?
Between us, a valley
of years I hadn't lived,
days full of doctors
who said I might die
if I didn't stop counting
almonds, days where
I couldn't bear
any green field or body
of water but craved
dry land, cacti
that bloomed red
from nothing.

Canto 15
In the Dusk

of that scene
Thelma says
you get what you settle for,
then blows a stream
of smoke towards Louise

Canto 14
I Traveled in a Spiral, I Never
Finished the Whole Perimeter

I sit underneath the magnolia tree,
but the hot pink blossoms bore me now.
They remind me of all the cuts I did not re-break
before the final bell, all the blood that could
have been. At closing time when most had gone
Coach leaned against the ropes,
lips brown from liquor. I hit her hard
because he said that's how you win
and I hit her until I remembered
it was him who was afraid—

Canto 14
Where I Haven't Gone

The new words arrive. They emerge from gaps
in time, do not stay in their
set circles. I grapple each verb, each noun
as if doing so could take back the punches
that split her cheek under my touch.
I regret, I regret, yes, I told myself
I would tell the truth here. I was good
at being good, at saying please and thank you
until it blackened another's cheek.

Canto 13
Both Words and Blood

I mean to say
I never wanted to leave this world,
but I left and left.
Each body I shed with diet,
remade with muscle—
were those a sin?
Each hem of skin
caught in bramble,
adorned the black cherries,
the oaks. I remember the nuns
above Bologna's corridors,
shaking out their sheets.

Canto 12
Stones, Which Oftentimes Did Move Themselves

I wanted to be watched,
to be told every step. If my back foot
angled at a wrong degree, my error
shuddered the ground and called
Coach forth. His knotted neck,
his ears pummeled into bloom.
My own command slowed into glue
somewhere along my spinal synapse
unlike the girls who worked the ring
like a chess board, who saw
every opponent's punch ahead of time.
One eye a telescope, the other
a microscope, I was no natural
but loved the cause to every error,
a symptom and then its diagnosis.
If a girl holds her breath
too long, a hook to the ear.
If she steps left when she should
have stepped right, an uppercut
to the low belly opens an aching bin.
What is the division
between a body and the rest of its life?
The stoplight learns to dim.

Canto 11
Upon the Margin

Underneath the boxing ring
there was another ring,
then another. I hit the heavy bag
so hard my back turned to knots.
There is a disease called
Angel Wing Syndrome—
to walk always as if in flight.
I was always fleeing to some healer
as if they could solve what
made me crave distillation:
to be caught in a jar
where I would melt
no invented wing.
A wise woman said
to heal, go deeper into yourself
but I was scared—when diving
into bright blue water, one's face must first
encounter the face reflected there—
eye to eye, that other side. I woke
most mornings sputtering
as the sun split Pisces over the horizon,
then hit the walls of my Astoria
shoe box room where I occasionally slept,
filled with pencils and scraps
from trying to map
everything out just so—
I know my rhumb lines,
I've done the work,
I've sat with myself in a quiet room.
But there I was again
with my rose of the wind,
my sandglass and spectacle.
A loxodrome appears straight
but is instead a spiral.

Canto 10
I Come Not of Myself

Victim once meant *holy exchange*
a white elephant gift for the gods—
who will get the box of goat's blood?
Who will get the girl torn from the mountain,
scraped up and swinging, yelling
come get me, motherfucker? I wanted to be nothing
less than a sideways sacrifice
for a God I'd never seen before except
for his shadow, which did not heel at his feet
but hooked a fishing line of black
into the lower back of my "subtle body."
That's what the healer said, clutching her gold
medallion so hard I thought the chain would break.
Every time I turned toward the sun, poured my coffee,
boarded a train—was it me
that moved? Or was I a marionette, strung with black rope?
Coach tugged and I tied my shoes.
brought a sandwich, unbuttoned my shirt—
At morning training, he said *you're strong,*
did you know that? I did not *know that* but I believed him
enough to drag back his crypt's
slate slab lid. Inside, all those girls—
I was one of them, you know.

Canto 10
Solve for Me That Knot

It is no small thing
to make a person feel no no no no no
like they can do anything. no no no no
Coach said *every person is a menu* no.
*i just pick what i want—*no no no no no no no
At the sports bar, his hand on my back,o—
hand, mitt, bullseye no no no no, no no no no no,
I aimed for as he caught o, no, no
the sweat flying off my neck. no no no no
Under the streetlight coming no no no no.
through the gym window no no
I shed diamonds of salt;o no no no no
I was buying time and drunk enough;
the whole world was rocking in colors. no no
He said I was purple and listen, I lied. no no.
I wanted to see. I said I saw o no no no no no, no no.
what floated around him, no no no, no no no no
how it changed depending on the hour.
Our. Aura once meant breath—*breathe* no no.
he said in his bed the same size as the ring,
still point of the turning world. no no no no no no no no,
I cradled his head in my lap. no no no no.
Imagined my body a coffin o no no no no no.
that could close around my dead o no
and keep it. I did. no no no no no no
                        no no no, no no.

Canto 10

no no no no no
no no no no no
no no no no no *no—*
no no *no no no no no*
no no no no no no—
no no no no, no no no no no,
no, no, no
no no no no no no
no no no no no no.
no no no
no no no no no
no no no no no;
no no no no no no no
no no no no no no no.
no no no no no no no no, no no.
no no no no. no no no no
no no no no,
no no no no no no no.
no. no no no no—*no*
no no no no no no no no no no no,
no *no no no no no.*
no no no no;
no no no no;
no no no no no no no.
no no no no no
no no no no no no
no no no. no no.

Canto 9
Holy Words All Confident

Arriving back home
I lowered into a bathtub of ice—
each shriek of cold,
each wrist wreathed in ache,
a clock that kept no time but kept me
out of the numinous room of sleep.
The mirror waited to greet me
but I did not want to see
the serpents flickering
through my hair,
eating their own tails
and naming themselves grief.
Or do I mean rage?
If I cut off a head,
one became two with
even longer teeth.
Their rattles shook
the anvil of my ear.
Still, I would not look. Reader, look
at what Medusa was punished for.

Canto 8
I Turned Toward the Sea of All Good Sense

The city I belonged to
existed only before morning's first
blue light. The daytime city I served
at brunch: their sleek bobs,
their dainty finger rings and pony-tailed
dogs. Into the restaurant came Tilda Swinton,
Radiohead, The Beastie Boys, Beyonce's manager.
They ordered tall glasses of green juice,
stabbed at their salads. All day the light clung
to their mulberry silk sheets, their baby
cashmere rugs. Fast motion through those hours,
the way the sun bleached a different
patch of the wall and flickered. I kept time
polishing the large glass windows, my hair slick with grease,
my lower back aching more each hour.
College boys came in, reeking of beer
on Sundays mornings just to use our bathrooms.
You're lying about eating here, I said to one,
poking him in the chest, almost crossing over—
but praise Lorenzo, who pulled a copper coin
from the drunk boy's ear and made him smile.
Praise, the city that let me in long after my shift,
long after the weights and the heavy bag
and the miles. The gym lights turned off
and I headed into the grey night
fingers flaked with iron. Click of horse's hooves
(or were those my heels?) as I looked for
neon red somewhere in Hell's Kitchen.
I wanted noise I could sit in without speaking,
for someone to approach and place the cold
of a beer bottle against the back of my neck.
All those tendons pulled tight. All those angels
scurrying back and forth. I kept waiting
for a messenger, someone who lived
in that other radiant city to bring me home,
 to open up the gates.

Canto 7
For with Unbroken Words They Cannot Say It

I wasn't alone in wanting to put
down what I carried.
The coach who lived in the crack house.
The coach who had been in jail.
The women who had been raped, assaulted,
lost children. The man with railroad
tracks up his arms. We found out these
things about each other slowly, carried them
until we collided. Take *this*, I would later say,
in a clinch with a woman who I had just met,
the spray of her sweat landing in my mouth
sour as skim milk, clashing with her *it*
without knowing exactly what it was:
heavy black balloon hovering
above us and everywhere.

The first day I showed up in French braids
with shoes shining, chewing on my plastic
bit. A coach that was not yet *Coach*
pulled open the ropes: *it's like teaching a toddler*
how to swim. we'll throw you
in there, you'll figure it out. I passed
through parted lips into shimmering air.
E. was waiting, 6 feet tall with abs so clear
I saw them split as she breathed—
inhale and the bell's pink bleed
pulled me into my wrists and neck,
single punch I knew. I thought all I had to do
was jab and my opponent would disappear,
but she kept coming forward as I leaned back
against the ropes, the plastic of her glove in my mouth,
my nose buzzing with pain that combed its way down
until I broke the first rule: I turned my back
and curled into a ball, a stone she could not
push—

(warbling of my throat
as I broke the second rule and wept)—
oil of my split lip and the prism of pain
that made every coach's face jump with
light. There's the person you think you are
and the person you are—
yes, I understand Tyson bit off a chunk of ear—
who in the ring doesn't show up
wanting to make an opponent submit
as if the opponent was their grief?
Chunk of flesh in the mouth: one way to speak.

Canto 6
Touching a Little on the Future Life

Long before New York I failed to edit
myself down to bone, sung *illium, sternum,*
scapula like spells but what gaped in me
opened further finally after all those years
of saying no. I left that small Maine town,
its ditches of snow, the dining halls where students
fed like cattle. After takeoff the stewardess
brought me bread and butter and I was above
the earth so I ate. The pasta: small capers
floating in a bloody sauce. Tiramisu
with a tiny spoon. I drank glass after glass
of red wine from a miniature cup.
Upon landing I felt a barking
come from below my three throats.
I could not yet speak that silken tongue
but I knew how to point—*I want.*
Voglio questo, fig gelato, cornetto filled with cream.
Quella, pasta with lemon zest, pizza
wide as a wheel. I ate it all.
I learned the words: *Avere fame.*
But I did not *have hunger,* as the Italians said—
I could not put it down.
I walked the market streets before
class and loaded up my baskets.
Above the red city the rains came
and I gave up the wisp that I was no longer.
I was blinded by bloat and I cringe
in the telling of the Italian nun
who painted my lips plum and said
there's a disorder you want and one you don't.
I couldn't understand but yes, I could.
Sciocchina, cosa fai qui? I shuttered my other life
and ate my way through the new.
In Matera I roamed the caves. I plucked figs
not yet ripe from the trees and ate them, too.

Canto 5
I Came into a Place Mute of All Light

Okay, fine, I wanted a *good* story.
I wanted a creation myth
folding in on itself like a
a tower of cards. I wanted silk robes
and a coach by my side,
for a crowd to cheer my
name. I wanted a new name,
I wanted forgiveness
so I did not have to forgive
the girl that I was all that time
I did not see the red thread I pulled
from a skein in the center
of my chest that always led
to the minotaur, a boy
who swam in rivers and beat himself
into sharp left hooks, mugs of wine,
pills that rattled his pocket like coins.

I, too, got lost in his rooms—
and of course! I wanted a body
bull-dozed into light
I couldn't source.
But beyond that,
nothing. No one could warn
me of me, how I wanted to hold
his horned head in my lap,
for his pronged tail to encircle me,
to tell me in which ring
I belonged

Canto 4
As It Seemed to Me from Listening

My other self I left
at the boxing gym's door.
She kept walking, husk
of a girl, and never looked back.
She crossed the street,
entered a bookstore,
ordered a cup of tea,
no caffeine. She was *good*,
is what I mean, and never woke
from slumber. No thunder clap
across the cheek. No blood tang
in the mouth, she slept on in the silence
of that other life and curdled,
red pen in hand. Her pages turned,
her phone blinked with its fishing hook
of blue. Mechanical maiden, is she aware of me
as she continues on?
She opened no door,
but kept walking into what she knew
and I, I walked inside—

Canto 3
To Commingle with the Coward Angels

For how many weeks did I dream of red?
For how many weeks did I dream my mouth
a rotted bud that would not bloom but bit?
I woke with my hands cross-stitched into fists.
Still it took 313 days for me to drive far
from the city's stationed smear.
For almost a year I entered no parks,
never turned on a stove. Inside the restaurant
where I worked: a merry-go-round of faces
blurred into needs, stained napkins.
I waited tables and paid rent
and did not write. The car was red.
I drove until I saw a field. Right up to the fence—
a foal, wearing a ring of blood like a crown,
eyes split open with light.
Anything can be an omen. Anything, a gate.
I was just going from one place to another
when I saw the boxing gym and walked in.
There was no river, no boat to take me across.
A clipboard, where I signed my name.
The man behind the desk smiled.
There are two kinds of people, he said,
those who come once and those who keep
coming back—which are you?
I did not walk down the basement steps
that day. I listened from above:
a bell, mitt against pad.
Someone's fists went: *whichwhichwhich*

Canto 2
And I, the Only One, Made Myself Ready to Sustain the War

And asked for help in the telling
because I'd already tried.
I tried to tell it in the voices
of other women. I tried to tell it
by way of prayer. I tried to tell it
by way of blessing, I tried to tell it
by way of blame. I tried to tell it small.
I tried to tell it sideways. I tried to tell it
slant. I tried to tell it silent. I tried to tell it
spit at a mirror. I tried to tell it broken.
I tried to tell it black eye. I tried to tell it
snapped wing, burst iris, yellow foundation.
I tried to tell it in 2nd person. I tried to tell it
with no person. I tried to tell it in sonnets.
I tried to tell it in ghazals. I tried to tell it erased.
I tried to tell it blown open. I tried never again
to tell it. Then I told it in Iceland. I told it in Italy.
I told it in Illinois. I told it in Virginia. I tried
to bury it in Virginia. I tried to leave it in Virginia.
I tried to begin again in Virginia. I tried to tell it
without entering. The only way was down.
Grip the railing, dear one.

Canto 1
How Hard a Thing It Is to Say

I was twenty two and starbright so
I did not see that I was lost. Who
wouldn't be—lost, I mean, in that city
of skyscrapers, blue-bearded men,
and no birds? Bluebirds I did not hear
for years—there were no trees.
There was no tiger or wolf or Beatrice.
There was no witch or wardrobe or someone
waiting. I packed my bags, said *I will be my Virgil*
in the story I could never quite begin.
Where to begin? My first week in New York
on that street (was it Broome?) a man yelled
you don't belong here, you smiling bitch
and I clomped on in my combat boots and
smiled even wider—I knew how to make a shape
out of me. For years I carved my ribs
myself. It's an old story, reader—
how I tallied calories
in the dark of sixteen. I did not know
what had come to take me
driven out of the mind into somewhere
sinew. A layer of hair grew as if to protect me
from myself. A body breaks down like any other—
I saw no flies but above me a small voice
pitched one octave higher than my own
spoke. It said: *whittle.*
I'd seen how carpenters
did it, their knives and spoons.
Quick scrape, the hollow,
then the light.

NOTES

"Esther" (page 12)
italicized line is from Psalms 114:5

"Purgatory" (page 27)
was inspired by Kiki Petrosino's "Afterlife."

Many of the titles in the last section are translated lines of the corresponding cantos from Dante Alighieri's *The Divine Comedy*. I referenced translations by Allen Mandelbaum and Henry Wadsworth Longfellow.

"Canto 10: Solve For Me That Knot" (page 60)
"still point of the turning world" is a quote from T.S. Eliot's "The Four Quartets."

ACKNOWLEDGMENTS

Versions of these poems first appeared in the following journals. Many thanks to their editors and readers.

Australian Book Review: "Before dawn, with the street lamp's beam across your face"
Beloit Poetry Journal: "Interview, Coach X."; "It does not matter"
December Magazine: "Melissa" (as "Rupture")
Pleiades Magazines: "How hard a thing it is to say" (as "I was 16")
The Common: "Circling the ring"; "Below the belt"
The Under Review: "Bless the Boxing Ring"; "Some things you can't understand by punching harder"

Thank you to the incredible women fighters I trained with. Your strength continues to astound me.

Thanks to Gabe Fried for your call about this prize as I stood in a field of snow, and for your attentive editing since. Gratitude to the rest of the team at Persea Books for their deep listening and careful eyes.

Thanks to Lexi Rudnitsky—may her memory be a blessing.

Thank you, Annyston, Alison, Benji, Cass, Eva, and Marie, who were my first readers, my first listeners, and who shaped this book with their hearts, minds, and unwavering support. I'm so glad I get to love you and write for you/with you.

Thanks to April, Janet, and Brea for bringing me back home to myself.

Thanks to the brilliant faculty (and visiting writers) at the University of Virginia's MFA program, who read many drafts of these poems. Kiki Petrosino, grazie mille for your steady wisdom and for being Glass Jaw's Virgil. Thanks to Rita Dove for teaching me that careful attention is a form of prayer, and to Lisa Russ Spaar for ecstatic language and Pisces insight. Special thanks to Barbara Moriarty and Jeb Livingood for keeping the ship afloat. And of course, thanks to my cohort (Hannah, Hodges, Jeddie, Kyle) and fellow poets at UVA—this book would have been very different without you.

Thank you to my new colleagues and teachers at Harvard Divinity School, who I am just beginning to know. Your hearts, minds, and support have already changed me.

Thanks to the Gullkistan Artist Residency, which offered a room filled with light in a snowy, dark winter. Thanks to Klara for whisking me away to Cinque Terre, and to Geneva for offering "a room of one's own" at Freedom House Farm. Molly, Emma, Erica, Roxanne, Jen, Sarah, and the Brooklyn Herborium women—thank you for your New York accompaniment. Annie, for being my favorite sparring partner and NYC guide. Thanks to Sarah P. for your life-giving artist dates.

Thanks to Phillips Exeter Academy for the abundance of space and time to dream and write and wonder, and to the town of Exeter, who welcomed me. A special thank you to Todd Hearon.

Thank you to my students, whose delight and curiosity gave me (and give me) great hope. Thank you to my many teachers and mentors across time, especially Rachel DeWoskin, Mina Marien, and Brock Clarke. Grazie mille to Arielle Saiber for sharing your enthusiastic, life-affirming love of Dante. Miigwech, Pat Cleveland—for poetry, for third grade, and every year since.

Thank you, Lake Michigan.

Thank you, Patti Smith, Joy Harjo, Aracelis Girmay, Lucille Clifton, and so many other artists and writers who have accompanied me.

Thanks to the many ancestors for their strength and survival. Thanks to my parents, Debra and Dave, and my brother Zane—such profound gratitude and love for you. To the rest of my family, writers and artists of past and present— your paintings, books, poker games, visits, phone calls, and cards have all bolstered me. Thank you for your humor and kindness, and for never blinking an eye when I said, "I want to be a poet when I grow up." I'm glad to be your kin.

Ilana, thank you for knowing, before I did, there was a way home through the mountains.

Derick, all that time, I was lucky enough to be living and writing towards you.

ABOUT THE LEXI RUDNITSKY FIRST BOOK PRIZE IN POETRY

The Lexi Rudnitsky First Book Prize in Poetry is a collaboration between Persea Books and The Lexi Rudnitsky Poetry Project. It sponsors the annual publication of a collection by a female-identifying poet who has yet to publish a full-length poetry book.

Lexi Rudnitsky (1972–2005) grew up outside of Boston. She studied at Brown University and Columbia University, where she wrote poetry and cultivated a profound relationship with a lineage of women poets that extends from Muriel Rukeyser to Heather McHugh. Her own poems exhibit both a playful love of language and a fierce conscience. Her writing appeared in *The Antioch Review, Columbia: A Journal of Literature and Art, The Nation, The New Yorker, The Paris Review, Pequod,* and *The Western Humanities Review*. In 2004, she won the Milton Kessler Memorial Prize for Poetry from *Harpur Palate*. Lexi died suddenly in 2005, just months after the birth of her first child and the acceptance for publication of her first book of poems, *A Doorless Knocking into Night* (Mid-List Press, 2006). The Lexi Rudnitsky First Book Prize in Poetry was founded to memorialize her and to promote the type of poet and poetry in which she so spiritedly believed.

PREVIOUS WINNERS OF THE LEXI RUDNITSKY FIRST BOOK PRIZE IN POETRY

2022   Shawn R. Jones, *Date of Birth*
2021   Anni Liu, *Border Vista*
2020   Sarah Matthes, *Town Crier*
2019   Sara Wainscott, *Insecurity System*
2018   Valencia Robin, *Ridiculous Light*
2017   Emily Van Kley, *The Cold and the Rust*
2016   Molly McCully Brown, *The Virginia State Colony for Epileptics and Feebleminded*
2015   Kimberly Grey, *The Opposite of Light*
2014   Susannah Nevison, *Teratology*
2013   Leslie Shinn, *Inside Spiders*
2012   Allison Seay, *To See the Queen*
2011   Laura Cronk, *Having Been an Accomplice*
2010   Cynthia Marie Hoffman, *Sightseer*
2009   Alexandra Teague, *Mortal Geography*
2008   Tara Bray, *Mistaken for Song*
2007   Anne Shaw, *Undertow*
2006   Alena Hairston, *The Logan Topographies*